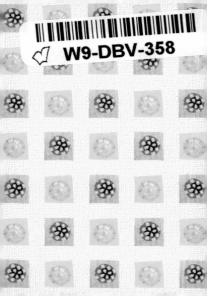

The Little Book of
WOMEN'S WISDOM

The Little Book of

WOMEN'S WiSDOM

ILLUSTRATIONS BY
MARIA CARLUCCIO

Lawrence Teacher Books
Philadelphia

Contents

INTRODUCTION

THE GIFT OF WISDOM STEMS FROM
the gift of life. Indeed, it is this simple. As we
live our moments, we grow, we learn, and we
strive for compassion. And there are those
among us who can capture the essence of a

Our True

Selves

IF NOW ISN'T
A GOOD TIME FOR
THE TRUTH
I DON'T SEE WHEN
WE'LL GET TO IT.

NIKKI GIOVANNI

AMERICAN POET (B. 1943)

moment, distilling a lesson learned or an ob-
servation keenly made into words that speak
to our hearts. These are the words — and the
wisdom — that enrich us, challenge us, and
make us glad.

This collection of wisdom from women,
both well-known and unknown, is filled with
insight and humor, love and yearning, lessons
and questions. Whether we concentrate on the

concrete—burping babies, the ocean, the bikini; or dawdle in the philosophical—the desire to do what is right, the often elusive state of grace, we recognize in their words our own musings, our own epiphanies. And sometimes, it shores us up to know that we are not alone in our thoughts, that we are among friends.

This book is full of the words of women who have searched for truth, their truth. In sharing their journeys with us, we are emboldened to continue on our own. And we do so with strength and laughter, believing that to be alive, to love and be loved, and to be a woman, all are gifts.

To enjoy yourself is
the easy method to give
enjoyment to others.

. . . .

L. E. LANDON

BRITISH POET, WRITER (1802–1838)

I've lived so long
because I get my rest
and I take my time.

. . . .

MARY THOMPSON

OLDEST LIVING AMERICAN WOMAN

Even with all my wrinkles!
I am beautiful.

. . . .

BESSIE DELANEY

AMERICAN DENTIST, WRITER

(1891–1995)

You know, don't you, that
the bikini is only
the most important thing
since the atom bomb.

. . . .

DIANA VREELAND

FRENCH-AMERICAN FASHION EDITOR

(1903–1989)

CLOTHES AND COURAGE HAVE SO MUCH TO DO WITH EACH OTHER.

SARA DUNCAN

CANADIAN WRITER (1861—1922)

I also think that
if we could get cellulite
put onto Barbie dolls,
it would help a lot with
self-acceptance.

....

SARK

20TH CENTURY AMERICAN WRITER

BEAUTY
WITHOUT GRACE
IS a HOOK
WITHOUT BAIT.

NINON DE L'ENCLOS
FRENCH SOCIETY FIGURE (1620–1705)

It all starts with self-reflection.
Then you can know and
empathize more profoundly
with someone else.

....

SHIRLEY MACLAINE

AMERICAN ACTOR (B. 1934)

One cannot exist today as a person—
one cannot exist in full
consciousness—without having a
showdown with one's self,
without having to define what it is that
one lives by, without being clear
in one's own mind what matters and
what does not matter.

....

DOROTHY THOMPSON

AMERICAN JOURNALIST, RADIO COMMENTATOR

(1894–1961)

Woman must
come of age by herself....
She must find
her true center alone.

. . . .

ANNE MORROW LINDBERGH
AMERICAN WRITER, AVIATOR (B. 1906)

We must overcome the notion
that we must be regular...
it robs you of the
chance to be extraordinary.

. . . .

UTA HAGEN

GERMAN ACTOR (B. 1919)

Never get so fascinated
by the extraordinary that
you forget the ordinary.

....

MAGDALEN NABB

BRITISH WRITER (B. 1947)

Cherish forever
what makes you unique,
'cuz you're really
a yawn if it goes!

. . . .

BETTE MIDLER

AMERICAN SINGER, ACTOR (B. 1945)

No one can dub you with dignity. That's yours to claim.

....

ODETTA

AMERICAN FOLK SINGER (B. 1930)

Without our
flaws, faults, and foibles,
we would be less lovable—
much less lovable.

....

SARK

20TH CENTURY AMERICAN WRITER

I long to tell you…
and listen as we
speak to each other
of what we know:
the light is in us.

....

SUSAN GRIFFIN

AMERICAN POET, WRITER (B. 1943)

There's a period of life
when we swallow
a knowledge of ourselves
and it becomes either
good or sour inside.

....

PEARL BAILEY

AMERICAN SINGER (1918–1990)

I was thought to be
"stuck up." I wasn't.
I was just sure of myself.
This is and always has been
an unforgivable quality
to the unsure.

. . . .

BETTE DAVIS

AMERICAN ACTOR (1908–1989)

STReNGTH

&

STRuGGLe

The only courage
that matters is the kind
that gets you from
one minute to the next.

....

MIGNON MCLAUGHLIN

AMERICAN WRITER (B. 1915)

I AM NOT
AFRAID OF STORMS
FOR i AM
LEARNING HOW TO
SAiL MY SHIP.

LOUISA MAY ALCOTT

AMERICAN WRITER (1832–1888)

The excursion is
the same when you go
looking for your sorrow
as when you go
looking for your joy.

. . . .

EUDORA WELTY

AMERICAN WRITER (B. 1909)

I weep a lot.
I thank God I laugh a lot, too.
The main thing in one's own
private world is to try to laugh
as much as you cry.

....

MAYA ANGELOU

AMERICAN POET, WRITER (B. 1928)

Life, for all its agonies . . .
is exciting and beautiful, amusing
and artful and endearing . . .
and whatever is to come after it—
we shall not have this life again.

. . . .

ROSE MACAULAY

BRITISH WRITER (1881–1958)

They say you should not
suffer through the past.
You should be able to wear
it like a loose garment,
take it off, and let it drop.

....

EVA JESSYE

AMERICAN CHORAL DIRECTOR (1895—1992)

I have sometimes been wildly,
despairingly, acutely miserable . . .
but through it all
I still know quite certainly that
just to be alive is a grand thing.

. . . .

AGATHA CHRISTIE
BRITISH WRITER (1891—1976)

Character cannot be
developed in ease and quiet.
Only through experiences
of trial and suffering can
the soul be strengthened,
vision cleared, ambition inspired,
and success achieved.

....

HELEN KELLER

AMERICAN WRITER, EDUCATOR (1880—1968)

The greater part of
our happiness or misery
depends on our
dispositions and not on
our circumstances.

．．．．．．．．．．．．．

MARTHA WASHINGTON

AMERICAN FIRST LADY (1719–1802)

Anger helps
straighten out a problem
like a fan
helps straighten out
a pile of papers.

. . . .

SUSAN MARCOTTE

20TH CENTURY AMERICAN WRITER

Patience, patience, patience,
is what the sea teaches.
Patience and faith.

. . . .

ANNE MORROW LINDBERGH

AMERICAN WRITER, AVIATOR (B. 1906)

ORDINARY WOMEN OF GRACE ARE, IN A SENSE, MY REAL ROLE MODELS.

MARIAN WRIGHT EDELMAN

AMERICAN CHILD ACTIVIST (B. 1939)

Life is a succession of
moments and to
live each is to succeed.

. . . .

SISTER CORITA KENT

AMERICAN ARTIST (1918—1986)

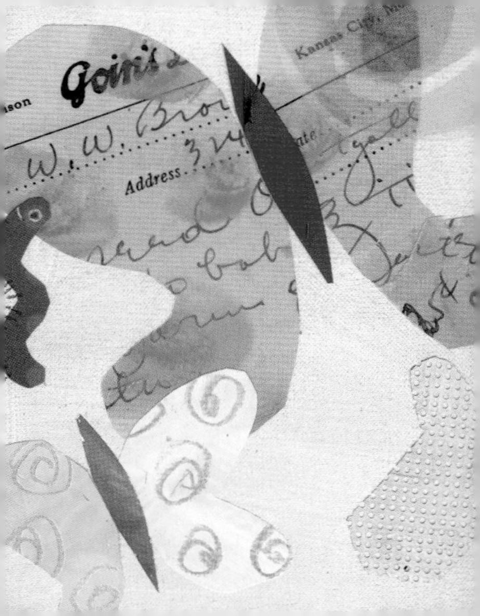
Kansas City,
Address

CoURAGe
········ TO ········
CHaNGE

I CANNOT
CHANGE THE
WORLD,
BUT I DO NOT
HAVE TO
CONFORM.

. . . .

MARVA COLLINS
AMERICAN EDUCATOR (B. 1936)

In knowing how to
overcome little things, a centimeter
at a time, gradually when
bigger things come, you're prepared.

. . . .

KATHERINE DUNHAM

AMERICAN DANCER (B. 1909)

I think the reward for
conformity is
that everyone likes you
except yourself.

. . . .

RITA MAE BROWN

AMERICAN WRITER (B. 1944)

You can focus on
the obstacles, or you can
go on and decide
what you do about it.

. . . .

GLORIA DEAN RANDLE SCOTT

AMERICAN EDUCATOR (B. 1938)

The strongest bulwark of
authority is uniformity;
the least divergence from it
is the greatest crime.

. . . .

EMMA GOLDMAN

AMERICAN ANARCHIST (1869—1940)

You have to be willing to
think the unthinkable.

....

TONI MORRISON

AMERICAN WRITER (B. 1931)

Progress always
involves risk.
You can't steal second
with your
foot on first.

. . . .

MARY R.

ANONYMOUS 20TH CENTURY AMERICAN WRITER

A GOOD MESSAGE WiLL ALWAYS FIND a MESSENGeR.

. . . .

ANN BEATTY

AMERICAN WRITER (B. 1947)

Avoiding danger is no
safer in the long run
than outright exposure.
Life is either a daring
adventure or nothing.

. . . .

HELEN KELLER

AMERICAN WRITER, EDUCATOR (1880–1968)

Any woman who can
stand her own company, can see
the beauty of the sunset,
loves growing things, and is willing
to put in as much time at
careful labor as she does over
the washtub, will certainly succeed.

. . . .

ELINORE RUPERT STEWART

EARLY 20TH CENTURY AMERICAN PIONEER

AND HOMESTEADER

The TRUTH is THAT PROGRESS is USUALLY SMALL AND SNeAky.

ANNE LAMOTT

AMERICAN WRITER (B. 1954)

Can't nothin'
make your life work if
you ain't the architect.

. . . .

TERRY MCMILLAN

AMERICAN WRITER (B. 1951)

In every human breast,
God has implanted a principle which
we call love of freedom;
it is impatient of oppression and
pants for deliverance.

. . . .

PHYLLIS WHEATLEY

AMERICAN POET (1753–1784)

Dissension is healthy,
even when it gets loud.

· · · · · · · · · · · · · ·

JENNIFER LAWSON

20TH CENTURY AMERICAN WRITER

One thinks like a hero
to behave like a merely
decent human being.

....

MAY SARTON

BELGIAN-AMERICAN WRITER (1912–1995)

If you are dissatisfied
with the way things are,
then you have got to
resolve to change them.

....

BARBARA JORDAN

AMERICAN POLITICIAN (1936–1996)

We can do
no great things;
only small things
with great love.

. . . .

MOTHER TERESA

FOUNDER, MISSIONARIES OF CHARITY

(1910–1997)

If women want any rights
more than they's got, why don't
they just take them,
and not be talking about it?

....

SOJOURNER TRUTH

AMERICAN PREACHER, ABOLITIONIST, WOMEN'S

RIGHTS ADVOCATE (1797—1883)

ANY TRUTH
CREATES
a SCANDAL.

. . . .

MARGUERITE YOURCENAR

FRENCH WRITER (1904–1988)

There is only one proof
of ability: action.

....

MARIE VON EBNER-ESCHENBACH

AUSTRIAN WRITER (1830—1916)

You should always know
when you're
shifting gears in life.

. . . .

LEONTYNE PRICE

AMERICAN OPERA SINGER (B. 1927)

LOVING

YOU LOSE
A LOT OF TIME
HATING PEOPLE.

MARIAN ANDERSON

AMERICAN SINGER, U.N. DELEGATE

(1902–1993)

One of the oldest
human needs is having
someone to wonder where
you are when you
don't come home at night.

. . . .

MARGARET MEAD

AMERICAN ANTHROPOLOGIST (1901–1978)

I always felt that the great
high privilege, relief, and comfort
of friendship was that
one had to explain nothing.

. . . .

KATHERINE MANSFIELD

BRITISH WRITER (1888—1923)

BUT IF LOVE IS
NOT THE CURE,
IT CERTAINLY CAN
ACT AS A VERY
STRONG MEDICINE.

KAY REDFIELD JAMISON

AMERICAN WRITER, PSYCHIATRIST (B. 1949)

Women must
know themselves before
they go out and
get into a relationship.

....

SONIA SANCHEZ

AMERICAN POET (B. 1934)

Love is or it ain't.
Thin love ain't love at all.

. . . .

TONI MORRISON

AMERICAN WRITER (B. 1931)

To love is not a state;
it is a direction.

. . . .

SIMONE WEIL

FRENCH PHILOSOPHER (1909–1943)

You are loved. If so, what else matters?

·············

EDNA ST. VINCENT MILLAY

AMERICAN POET (1892–1950)

The Gift

······ OF ······

CHiLDReN

Women are strong, strong,
terribly strong.
We don't know how strong
we are until we're
pushing out our babies.

. . . .

LOUISE ERDRICH

CHIPPEWA-AMERICAN WRITER (B. 1954)

Making the decision
to have a child—it's momentous.
It is to decide forever to
have your heart go walking around
outside your body.

. . . .

ELIZABETH STONE

AMERICAN WRITER (B. 1946)

Truth, which is important to
a scholar, has got to be concrete.
And there is nothing
more concrete than dealing with
babies, burps, and bottles.

. . . .

JEANNE J. KIRKPATRICK

AMERICAN DIPLOMAT (B. 1926)

DON'T FORGET
THAT COMPARED TO
A GROWNUP
PERSON EVERY
BABY IS A GENIUS.

MAY SARTON

BELGIAN-BORN AMERICAN WRITER (1912–1995)

boursday   ball

They love you to
tell them how great they are,
how good they are.
Somehow, even at a young age,
they understand that.

....

CLARA MCBRIDE HALE

AMERICAN CHILD ACTIVIST (1905–1992)

It is a beautiful enough
shock to fall in
love with another adult....
But love of an infant
is of a different order.

. . . .

LOUISE ERDRICH

CHIPPEWA-AMERICAN WRITER (B. 1954)

LiFE

LESSoNS

The GREATEST LESSON In LIFE IS THAT YOU ARE RESPONSIBLE FOR YOUR OWN LIFE.

OPRAH WINFREY

AMERICAN ACTOR (B. 1954)

The art of life is not
controlling what
happens to us, but using
what happens to us.

....

GLORIA STEINEM

AMERICAN ACTIVIST, WRITER, EDITOR (B. 1934)

The quality of our laughter
and joy, the knowledge of our voices,
thoughts, and actions are weaving
beauty around the land.

....

DHYANI YWAHOO

20TH CENTURY NATIVE AMERICAN WRITER

Life shrinks or expands
in proportion
to one's courage.

....

ANAIS NIN

FRENCH-AMERICAN WRITER

(1903—1977)

It's when we're given choice
that we sit with the gods
and design ourselves.

....

DOROTHY GILMAN

AMERICAN WRITER (B. 1923)

You grow up the day
you have the first real
laugh—at yourself.

....

ETHEL BARRYMORE

AMERICAN ACTOR (1879–1959)

The ultimate of being successful
is the luxury of
giving yourself the time to do
what you want to do.

. . . .

LEONTYNE PRICE

AMERICAN OPERA SINGER (B. 1927)

CREATIVITY CAN BE DESCRIBED AS LETTING GO OF CERTAINTIES.

....

GAIL SHEEHY

AMERICAN JOURNALIST, WRITER (B. 1937)

Nothing in life
is to be feared.
It is only to
be understood.

....

MARIE CURIE

POLISH-BORN FRENCH PHYSICIST

(1867–1934)

The first problem for all of us,
men and women,
is not to learn, but to unlearn.

. . . .

GLORIA STEINEM

AMERICAN ACTIVIST, WRITER, EDITOR

(B. 1934)

The mind loves to
not know completely....
To get smarter,
do the unfamiliar.

. . . .

MAGALY RODRIGUEZ MOSSMAN

20TH CENTURY AMERICAN WRITER

EARTH'S CRAMMED WITH HEAVEN.

ELIZABETH BARRETT BROWNING

BRITISH POET (1806–1861)

People see God every day,

they just

don't recognize him.

. . . .

PEARL BAILEY

AMERICAN SINGER (1918—1990)

It is good to have
an end to journey towards,
but it is the journey
that matters in the end.

. . . .

URSULA LEGUIN

AMERICAN WRITER (B. 1929)

To practice magic is
to bear the responsibility for
having a vision, for we
work magic by envisioning
what we want to create.

. . . .

STARHAWK

AMERICAN WRITER, LECTURER (B. 1951)

IF YOU'RE NOT LIVING ON THE EDGE, YOU'RE TAKING UP TOO MUCH ROOM.

LORRAINE TEEL

AMERICAN ACTIVIST (B. 1951)

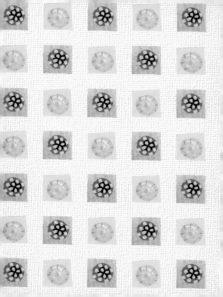